Closer to God
Simple Methods, Starting Today

SHERRY ELAINE EVANS

When you draw near to God, His Spirit draws near to you. — Sherry
James 4:8

©2017
GOSPEL LIFE PUBLISHING

Copyright © 2017 by Sherry Elaine Evans

All Rights Reserved

Published in the United States by Gospel Life Learning, Spring, TX

Book design by Gospel Life Learning

Cataloging-in-Publication Data

Evans, Sherry Elaine

    Closer to God: Simple Methods, Starting Today

    p. 100

    Summary: Simple methods for prayer and journaling and motivation for

        living life closer to God.

.

ISBN: 9781976804069

AISN: B078S23DBZ

Dedicated to my daughters,
Meghan and Maddie.

Contents

Introduction: Meet Anne..................................7

Chapter 1: The Realization.............................9

Chapter 2: A Simple, Effective Method of Prayer #1..................................18

Chapter 3: A Simple, Effective Method of Prayer #2..................................29

Chapter 4: A Simple, Effective Method of Prayer #3, Prayer with Journaling........38

Chapter 5: A Simple Effective Method #4, Keeping God in Mind, Through Jesus......54

Chapter 6: Motivation to Pray............................62

Chapter 7: Powerful Prayers and Powerful Faith...73

Resources 78

About the Author 84

Excerpts from *He Called* 86

Introduction: Meet Anne

This short book tells of a transformation that occurred one year in the life of a young woman named Anne. The year was 2012, so it was not that long ago.

See, prior to 2012, Anne had a problem with her walk with God. She was still living too far from Him in her daily life. She lacked closeness with God, even though she thought that she had tried to do many things to find and maintain closeness with Him over many years. Anne had started to believe that there must just be certain types of people who were able to "be and feel" close to God; and she just wasn't one of those people. She was disappointed, and she longed to have the deep friendship with God as she saw others have. Yet, it just didn't seem to happen for her.

Anne seemed to have many reasons and numerous obstacles in her way, blocking her relationship with the Lord.

> She always became really distracted in prayer.

> She almost completely forgot about God most days, especially when she was working or busy.

> There had been a time in her past when she was withholding a secret area of disobedience towards God in her life, and she felt like perhaps she would never find closeness to Him because of it.

> She could read her Bible, but it just didn't seem to "speak to her heart" at all.

This all changed for Anne, however, once she began truly seeking friendship with the Lord and determined to seek it with all her heart. First she was inspired, and next she began to seek and to consult with others to help her in her spiritual growth.

This little book is not going to be filled with long, drawn out hypothetical scenarios.

It is not going to discuss the philosophy of the human mind, nor the wonder of the God to Man relationship.

This book won't go into the theology of spiritual warfare; and it won't even delve into all the benefits of prayer.

This book is for any Christian who recognizes that he or she wants to walk closer with God. This book will quickly address the roots of the problems which hinder our closeness – our motivation, our lack of knowledge of His promises; our busyness, and our lack of focus – and it will offer simple strategies and routines for the purpose of bringing our daily lives back in communion with God.

For Anne, the teachings in this book led her to a deep closeness with God for the first time, in a way that she had not yet experienced before.

For you, the reader:
 Enjoy the pages, and enjoy the closeness of the Lord, which I pray you should discover and maintain through its short and helpful pages.

1

The Realization

On a rainy Wednesday evening, Anne, a young mother, parked her car in the church parking lot, finding a place within sprinting distance from the covered walkway leading to the doors of the building. Exiting the car while simultaneously opening a large umbrella, Anne turned to the back passenger side of the car, where she unlatched the two year old baby girl from the car seat, and then carefully transferred the baby to a portable stroller. She continued to balance the large umbrella over their heads. Anne then reached across the backseat of the car and unlatched her four year old daughter from her booster seat, and then led the older sister by the hand out of the car. "Let's go! Let's go!" She called out to the young girls. "Stay close! Stay under the umbrella if you can!" Rain pelted against their arms and legs, and droplets plopped against the top of the umbrella. Anne and the preschooler scurried, as she pushed the stroller, as quickly as they could, until they arrived under the covered walkway and then entered the church doors.

"We made it! Let's go find your classrooms," Anne spoke, pushing the stroller and leading the four year old down the hallway to the children's rooms, where every Wednesday evening church staff members and volunteers provided free childcare and free children's programming for an hour while their parents attended the midweek evening service. Anne, a young, working mother, came to church nearly every Wednesday evening. She had been doing so since shortly after her second daughter was born. This midweek service actually offered more than just as church service to her. It offered a full hour each week during which she could sit in the sanctuary and rest, while others watched her children. The worship singing during the first fifteen minutes of each services was often uplifting and relaxing too.

Once the sermon started, Anne would quickly assess whether or not this was a message similar to any that she had heard before. If so, she could merely zone out and let her mind rest. Every once in awhile the sermon was truly inspiring; but most Wednesdays she found the message to be a repeat of something she had already heard many times before. After all, Anne had been attending church regularly since she was a child. However, the mid-week service still gave her time to rest while someone else took care of the young children, wiped their sticky fingers, fed them a snack, and supervised their play on the playground – an indoor playground! She went to church nearly every Wednesday night, even rainy Wednesday nights, because her young girls loved the indoor playground and because it gave her a nice hour of respite in the middle of a hectic week of work and family responsibilities.

Anne found a seat in the sanctuary, not too far up front, but not too far back either. She participated in the worship singing. It was a really nice set of songs that evening – including one of her favorites, "Open the Eyes of My Heart." Anne had made sure she was far enough back not to be noticed should she not be paying attention. Sometimes she even brought a book to read during the sermon if it wasn't a topic she felt she needed to hear.

Dr. Trammell, the pastor, approached the podium and started, "I'm going to start reading from James 4, and I want you to help me finish this verse. Are you ready? 'Draw near to God, and – '"

He paused mid-sentence; then he began again, "Draw near to God, and....what comes next?" Let's say it together."

Nearly every member in the congregation that evening called out, "*And he will draw near to you.*"

The pastor smiled and encouraged them, "Let's finish it again! Draw near to God, AND..."

"*He will draw near to you!*" The congregation called back, with increased enthusiasm.

Anne's heart fluttered and warmed in her chest. She had heard that verse before, many times before. After all, Anne was raised by Christian parents, even raised in Christian schools, and even attended a large Christian college. Anne had prayed for Jesus to come into her heart at a very young age. She then re-dedicated her life to Christ in middle school during a church retreat. She had attended church sporadically even as a college student and a young single adult. After she married, she and her husband joined a large church and attended nearly every weekend. They had made many friends in the church, and they felt like they were growing more spiritually. Now, Anne was attending on Wednesday evenings too – but mainly for the respite, not because she truly desired or felt she needed to hear another sermon.

Anne had most certainly heard that verse before. However, this time it was different.

Draw near to God, and He will draw near to you.

Anne had studied the English language; so she knew this

verse was a command; at least it started as a command. Before, Anne had always focused on the first part of the verse, the part that is a command, the part that commanded her to "Draw near to God."

For the first time; however, Anne saw the promise in the verse. It was a spiritual truth, a spiritual promise, perhaps even a spiritual law. If anyone does A; that person will receive B. If anyone draws near to God, then God will draw near to that person.

That night, Anne realized that even though she was at church nearly every weekend,

and even though she had been born into a Christian home,

and even though she prayed for Jesus to come into her heart at a young age;

and even though she was baptized when she was in the sixth grade;

she realized that she had never recognized this amazing promise from God.

Even though she had checked off the boxes and was doing all the things she thought she should be doing, she was *not* living close to God.

Perhaps that was why deep down, she felt as if she was living day after day, going through the motions. Perhaps that is why she often felt as if she was trapped on a train of life, looking out the window as the landscapes passed by, wondering what it was that she was missing.

The verse presented that night was James 4:8. Some versions say, "Come close to God, and He will come close to you."

Anne was one of millions of people who consider themselves to be a follower of Christ, yet they don't know God's presence in their lives. These millions of people are good people. They are striving to live a "Christian life." Yet, they don't feel the closeness of the Spirit of God. They may not even know that there are ways to be close to God.

Anne was one of those millions that Wednesday, rainy evening when she entered the church building.

However, over the next several months she learned another mystery of God, straight from the pages of His word. Anne learned that God proclaims, "Am I a God who is only close at hand?" says the LORD. "No, I am far away at the same time." (NLT)

God is both close and far at the same time. How can that be?

That night, Anne discovered this truth. God is close to those who draw near to Him, to those who call upon Him in faith. However, for those who are not coming to Him, His help remains far. *God is far from those not seeking Him, even though, ironically, He is near and available to them, as soon as they have a change in heart towards Him.*

We have to realize, like Anne did, that the Bible never promises that God will always be close and ready to help those of us who "got saved" on a retreat when we were young, yet haven't given Him much thought since then. It doesn't say God is close to those who call themselves a Christian. It doesn't even say that He is close and ready to strongly help those who regularly go to church. Instead, God is close to those who are drawing close to Him.

We are able to see this promise not only in James 4:8, but also in many other places throughout the Biblical narrative. Psalms 145:18 tells us that "The Lord is near to <u>all</u> who call upon Him." We should carefully analyze those words. Does it say that the Lord is near to all the hundreds of millions who call themselves a Christian? Does it say the Lord is near to all those who have good intentions in their hearts? No. The Lord is near to <u>all</u> who call upon Him.

We find this truth again in Zechariah's prophecy, "Return to me, says the Lord....so that I may return to you." (Zech 1:3). We hear that the Lord begs his people to come back to Him. He wants to be near to them; *but they have to move towards Him first.* He wants to strongly help them. He wants to guide them and protect them. He wants to lead them towards fulfilling lives.

We also can find this poetic promise: "The Lord's eyes keep on roaming throughout the earth, looking for those whose hearts completely belong to him, so that he may <u>strongly support</u> them." We discover this amazing spiritual truth in 2 Chronicles 16:9. We realize now that this promise is made over and over again. Who is God wanting to strongly support? Answer: Those whose hearts are near to His.

We then return to the New Testament where the writer in Hebrews 6 assures us, "...He <u>rewards</u> those who <u>earnestly</u>

seek Him." We now cannot deny the spiritual truth that the Lord helps and even rewards those who are drawing close to Him.

When Anne fully realized that she could ensure the Lord's nearness through her own faithful action of seeking to be near to Him, it transformed her spiritual life and her walk with the Lord.

Suddenly, Anne didn't want to read her Bible just for knowledge; she wanted to read it and ponder it for the purpose of keeping His Spirit close!

Anne no longer wanted to pray merely to send up requests which she hoped He would answer to her desired outcome. Instead, Anne began desiring to pray more frequently than ever, about every little thing she could possibly come up with to pray about. She wanted to pray frequently, all throughout the day. She was motivated to do this to ensure His nearness!

Before, Anne was honestly doing good to complete a genuinely sincere prayer even once a week.

After, Anne began setting reminders for ways to help her think about God throughout the day. She began keeping a prayer journal, sometimes filling three or more pages a day of both small and large requests, as well as many notes of thanksgiving.

Do you know what happened?

God came near to Anne. Just as the Bible had told her that He would.

He came near enough for Anne to practically feel His presence at times. He came near enough to answer nearly every single one of her many prayer requests that began filling pages and pages in her journal. He came so near and helped her in countless small and large ways.

Ultimately, Anne's faith in His existence and in His personal willingness to help went from being strong, to being rock solid strong, to being absolutely unshakeable.

Anne's prayer journal became evidence not only of His Spirit's existence, but also for the journal's abundant evidence that proved that He stays near to those who stay near to Him.

And now, to close this first chapter, a confession must be revealed. Anne's story is my own story. The real Anne is me, the author of this little book titled *Closer to God: Simple Methods, Starting Today.* I invite you to come along with me through the rest of these pages, and let me share more with you more about how Anne's walk with the Lord was transformed. I mean, let me tell you, through the character of Anne, how my walk with God was transformed

Your walk with God, too, will transform once you fully understand these few mysterious but simple spiritual truths that Anne discovered. When you learn simple, effective methods for drawing near to God; you can be confident that He is also drawing close to you. As it has been said, the truths are simple, but the actions and habits are not always simple to implement. However, Anne found a number of simple and effective methods for keeping close to God. These methods are explained for you further in the following pages of this book, available for any of us who desire more of the Lord's presence in our lives.

2

A Simple, Effective Method of Prayer

Now that you have met Anne, I want to share with you how her life changed over the next several months, and how she remained closer to God throughout the following years. Anne went from merely going through the motions to truly living life close to God.

First, Anne knew that prayer is the best avenue for communicating with God and experiencing a close relationship with God. And therein was her first major problem. Anne knew that, if she was honest with herself, then she would have to admit that she was bad at praying.

She was *really* bad at praying.

Praying for longer than a minute or so was not something that Anne had done often, and it did not come naturally to her. The truth is, prayer does not come naturally to most of us. We become distracted and often don't even finish our prayers. Often, we may not even remember all that we had prayed about just the day before. And if we are truly honest, many of our prayers are nothing more than requests to God. "God please, please, do this or please do that!"

However, like Anne, we now realize that prayer is not just a spiritual discipline or a spiritual practice. In other words, it is not something that we are just "supposed to do" as a Christian practice. Rather, Anne now understood that prayer is an act that would bring her closer to God; and when she intentionally drew near to God, God then would draw near to her.

Remember this: When we pray, we are close to God, and He is close to us. This is why we pray. We pray because authentic prayer keeps God close to us; prayer draws God's attention to us. When we authentically pray regularly, it brings God's available support into our lives. Simply put, prayer brings God into our lives!

Anne recognized that she needed to turn her stale, obligatory prayers into authentic prayer. To start, she determined to discover a simple, *effective* method of prayer.

The Simple, Effective Four Step Method of Prayer

Luckily, Anne learned such a simple, effective prayer method from one of her pastors. Anne began using this prayer method in order to greatly improve her prayer life. She began having more effective prayers and more focus in prayer. Anne was surprised to learn this simple method of prayer. She had been going to church for so many years, yet she hadn't learned this before. The method she learned is the method that I will explain in the rest of this chapter.

We truly struggle with consistent prayer. *We also struggle with focused prayer.* We sometimes wonder why our prayers don't seem effective. Much of the time we feel like our prayers are "hitting the ceiling." We may honestly doubt whether or not God truly hears our prayers, and we aren't always sure if He really cares about our specific situations.

After starting to use this effective prayer method, as well as the other methods that will be explained in later chapters, Anne truly came to realize that prayer truly is effective and powerful, especially when it is prayed by a person who is genuinely walking with God.

This simple, effect method of prayer consists of four main steps.

The <u>first step</u> has two parts, and the two parts are *Praise* and *Thanksgiving*. When we begin our prayer, we start the prayer by thanking and praising God for who He is and then thanking Him for what He has done. We learn to begin the prayer with praise to Him, in recognition of who He is and His characteristics. Here are some examples of how we may start our prayers.

Lord, I praise you for your faithfulness.
I praise you because you created me and know all about me.
Thank you God, for always being near.
Thank you, for working out your plan for us.
Thank you for your promises to provide.
Thank you for being greater that any problem I may have.
Thank you.........
Thank you.........
Thank you.........

When we begin our prayers in such a manner, with thankfulness to the Lord, we recognize that our hearts are "being set" in the right condition for approaching God. It also helps to release any anxiety we may be carrying over the response or answer to our prayers.

Next in prayer, we learn to confess in the prayer. Typically, we always have some sins that will come right to mind. After we confess the sins that easily come to mind, we will then ask God to help bring to mind anything specific we need to confess. For me, I often find myself holding onto sinful attitudes or grudges, and during this time, I will ask God to help reveal any attitudes or grudges or bitterness within me that I should confess. Then, after each confessed each sin, we will pray in this way: "*I confess _____, and I accept your forgiveness.*" Most of us have never prayed confession in that way before, and immediately we will begin to notice a difference. Some report that they feel something like a physical lifting away of the burden of their sins when praying in this manner.

The reason confessing in this way is important and recommended, is due to the fact that the Bible tells us this important truth: *If* we confess our sins, *He* will forgive them. This is another spiritual truth, God's truth:

If we confess, then He forgives it. It's another spiritual law. If we do A; God will do B. If we draw near to God; he will draw near to us. If we confess our sin, he will forgive our confessed sin.

Truly, if we confess, with an authentic and contrite heart and a desire to repent -- He will forgive it! It is done! Forgiven!

However, what many of us normally do is this: We find ourselves confessing the same thing over and over to God in our individual prayers. On Monday we make a confession; and then on Tuesday we confess the same thing again, and then the next day we are still confessing the same thing again. *When we do this, when we keep confessing the same sin over and over, we are keeping ourselves stuck in place with God.* God will forgive us for each sin confessed. That is His promise. *So when we confess each sin, immediately after, verbally accept the forgiveness that He provides.* This helps to break the cycle of guilt that we heap upon ourselves, and it frees us to continue walking forward with God, with a true appreciation for the fact that we are fully forgiven.

Here is an example: "Lord, I got really angry, and I was extremely rude. I am sorry. I confess my wrong attitude about _____. I want you to help me change, *and I accept your forgiveness.*" We will realize that c*onfessing and accepting* in this way releases our burdens and angst over past sins. We can now take hold of His promise and joyfully know that "He's forgiven me! Truly, He's forgiven me." We can move ahead in our relationship towards God and with God. We move closer to Him, rather than remaining stuck in the same dry and familiar spiritual place.

Lord, I confess that I (specific sinful action); *and I accept your forgiveness.*
I confess my (specific sinful attitude); and I ask you to help me change, *and I accept your forgiveness.*

Lord, I confess my (specific sinful thoughts); *and I accept your forgiveness.*

Next, after praying out the first phase of thanksgiving and the second phase of confession, next we learn to move into the <u>third portion</u> of the prayer, which is when we make requests to God. This is the easy part of prayer. I've never had to teach anyone how to make requests to God. We already know how to make prayer requests to God, to ask Him for help or for guidance. So during the third part of the prayer, we make our requests to God – requests for ourselves and for others.

Finally, in the <u>fourth step</u>, we learn to close each prayer with telling God that, regardless of our own desires, we want His will to be done. I usually close my prayers with something such as this: *"This is what I want; I really hope that this is within your will; but Lord, if it is not, I know that somehow – your plan is what is best for me."*

At first, we may not be comfortable closing prayers in such a way; however, over time, we realize that God's ways are often better than our own ideas. We also will notice that when we close our prayers in such a way, and truly mean it, that we seemed to release much of any anxiety we may be holding over the requests. By closing our prayers in this manner, we are telling the Lord, "I am giving it to You; and I trust You to do what is best for all involved." It can be very difficult to let go of the outcome of prayer given to God in this manner; but over time, God truly does work through it all for His purposes which are good purposes.

To summarize, here are the four steps in this simple, effective prayer method:

1) Begin prayer with thanks and praise to God
2) Next, confess to the Lord all that comes to mind, *and intentionally accept His forgiveness.*

3) Third, make your requests to God – for yourself and for others.

4) Finally, close your prayer by authentically releasing the outcome of the prayer to God's will and his plan. Let God know you will accept the result, whether the prayer is answered as you requested or not, because you trust His plan is best.

Method for Keeping Focused in Prayer

Anne was grateful to have learned such a simple and effective method of prayer to improve her prayer life and her communication with God. *However, even after learning and implementing these four simple steps, she still struggled with not being able to focus for long in her prayers.* She still found her mind in scattered, or distracting thoughts would intrude into her prayers. Oftentimes she felt so tired during night prayers that she would nearly fall asleep. However, Anne discovered a solution to this prayer problem, a problem that is common to nearly everybody. The suggestion came from one of Anne's friends. The suggestion was another simple, effective method to keep focused in prayer. Anne applied her friend's suggestion, and it worked fantastically! The suggestion was this:

> Set a 1 minute timer at the beginning of your prayer time. Spend that first minute in prayer and thanksgiving to God. If you need more time for giving thanks, then quickly reset the timer for another minute. After the first part of the prayer, the thanksgiving portion, tap the reset area on the timer for another minute. Then begin your time of confession. Continue with resetting the timer in one minute intervals, until you are finished with your prayer and time with God.

At first, many people may not be sure if they are comfortable with the suggestion of using the timer. Anne also wasn't sure about the idea, at first. We might think that using a timer will make the prayer feel forced, or robotic, or unauthentic. However, by using a simple digital timer, like the ones that now come standard on nearly every smart phone, we can set the timer to sound as a soft buzz or vibration. So do try this suggestion and see what happens with your level of focus during prayer. Set the timer to sound as a soft buzz or vibration. Then set the timer for one minute and press "Start." Then begin praying the first part of the prayer – the thanksgiving portion of the prayer.

When Anne first tried this suggestion, she prayed lists of thankfulness for a full minute, and she was surprised at how focused she was during just that minute. She was focused because she knew the timer was going to sound off to signal her to move to the next portion of the prayer. When the timer buzzed quietly, she quickly hit the reset button, and began praying the confession portion of the prayer. Anne confessed her sins and wrong attitudes, and she verbally accepted His forgiveness. Anne also asked God to help bring things to her mind that she needed to change. The timer went off, and Anne wasn't finished with all of her needed confession! So she quickly hit the reset area on her phone, and she kept praying out her confessions to the Lord. Anne confessed each thing that came to her mind and then she prayed, "I accept your forgiveness" after each. She had to quickly reset the timer three times in order to finish all the confession that came to her mind. Anne learned that by praying with the support of a soft-sounding timer to keep her on track, she was able to become so focused that she also became more thoroughly convicted and moved by the spirit of God during this time.

The simple timer trick is really working and helping many others with their focus in prayer with God! It isn't the timer itself that is helping the prayer. *The timer is helping our ability to focus in prayer.* Others have reported that it actually doesn't feel forced or unauthentic at all. In fact, by using the structure of the prayer and the timer strategy, we usually find ourselves craving more minutes and more time in prayer with God. Simply put, when we are more focused in prayer we are closer to God. We are drawing near to Him; and He will be drawing near to us.

We then continue our timer-based prayer that and move into the third portion of the prayer, the part where her requests were made. We are able to hand off our concerns and desires to the Lord, and we likely will be so focused that we need to reset the timer for several minutes. Then we close the prayer by authentically and honestly saying to

God, "Lord, this is what I ask; however, I want what you want more. I know your plans are best."

For clarification, this is not a suggestion to set a one minute timer for each part of the prayer to result in a prayer that is always four minutes long. The purpose of the timer is to help keep you focused. There is something about knowing that the timer will sound soon, that keeps the mind more focused. Anne chose to set her timer in one minute intervals; but if she needed more time at any point during the prayer, she could easily add more time by pressing the reset button. You can choose to set your timer in two or three minute intervals if you wish.

The first time I used the soft-sounding timer to support my prayer, I closed the prayer after nearly eight minutes of focused time with the Lord. As I continued to use the timer strategy, I found that my prayers were actually more extended in time, more authentic, more focused, and closer in spirit to the Lord. I learned that when one is focused in prayer, one requires, desires, and naturally finds more time to spend with God, not less. Finally, when we are spending focused, quality time, close to God, then our prayers become effective.

Closing Thoughts on Confession in Prayer

Before we close out this chapter, let's look at some reasons and some Biblical teaching on why it is very important to have a time of confession in our daily prayer. This is often the most difficult part of prayer for us, as it is a time of being genuine and honest and contrite before the Lord. ***The Bible tells us that confession is important is in order***

for us to be near to God and for God to be able to most effectively guide us:

In James 4:1-7, we are told that when we are in an ongoing state of daily confession, the devil will flee from us. Therefore, by maintaining a habit of confession, sin and temptation cannot maintain a grasp in our lives!

In Mark 11:25, we are told to forgive and release the grudges we have against others, and to do this at the beginning of our confession time. So we first confess any grudges or unforgiveness we are holding in our heart against others. When we forgive others; He is able to fully forgive us. For this reason, we pray our confession, accept His forgiveness, and then make our requests to God. Our prayers may not be as effective as the could be, if we have not confessed areas of unforgiveness in our lives.

In Acts 2:38, we are clearly told that we must *confess and repent* to receive the Holy Spirit.

In Hosea 14:1, it is prophesied that the people of God will stumble if they remain in their iniquity - in a state of non-confession. So how do we escape from our iniquity? We do so through ongoing confession.

3

A Simple, Effective Method of Prayer #2
Praying the Psalms

There is also another helpful method of prayer, much different from the first. This second type of prayer is especially helpful, because in this type of prayer, we don't even have to come up with things to pray about. The method is often referred to as "praying the scripture." There are several other books and resources available which explain this method; however, the one that appeals most to me, at least for starting out, is a method based on reading and praying the Psalms.

We will discover that when we begin praying the scriptures, it feels as if we are actually receiving God's word into our prayer life. The first method we learned in the last chapter, the simple four step method, provides us with a scaffold for breathing our own words out to God. In this second method, we may feel as if we are breathing in God's word into our spirits, as if we are breathing His words and His truths into the prayer.

Sometimes we find ourselves in a place where we need to talk to God, but not merely to worship, to confess, to ask, or to "let go." Sometimes we want to spend time with God merely to be refreshed by Him, to be inspired by Him, to be renewed by Him, and to be reassured by Him.

To pray this way, we begin by reading the Psalms, and

then actually "inserting ourselves" into the Psalm by praying from a point of view that mirrors the psalmist writer's point of view. We begin by reading through the Psalms until we find a particular passage that prompts us to pray. It usually doesn't take too long, as each Psalm can contain so much emotion and desire for the Lord. We don't have to have a specific plan for deciding which Psalm we will choose on any certain day. Instead, we can just relax and begin reading through the Psalms until we come upon a passage which inspires us to pray. We then mark this place in our Bible with a simple bookmark; and the next time we desire to pray with the Psalms, we may pick up wherever we left off prior, and we will continue to read in the Psalms until we come to another passage that again inspires us to pray through it.

Here is an example of how I might do this. On one particular day, I started where I had left off before in the Psalms, and I read to Psalms 37. In Psalms 37:1, I read this:

Fret not yourself because of evildoers;
be not envied of wrongdoers!
For they will soon fade like the grass
and wither like the green herb.

Trust in the Lord, and do good;
dwell in the land and befriend faithfulness.
Delight yourself in the Lord, and he will give you the
desires of your heart.

These words inspired something in me; and I wished to pray through these vesers. I re-read the section more carefully, and then asked myself, "What if I were speaking these words, or themes, to God today? How would I say these words? How would I put it into my context in my life today?" I thought about those questions, and then line by line, I turned the prayer of David into my own prayer. So for the passage above, I prayed something like this:

Oh God! I see so much bad in the world – so much evil! Remind me not to fret about it! And certainly Lord, I do not ever want to have the desire to join in on it.
Thank you Lord that you have a plan in place, and in that plan evil will fade away.
It's time will be short, like the length of life of a daylily, when compared to the length of eternity I will spend fully with You.

Lord, help me to always trust in You, Lord. Help me to do good and to think good.
Help me to be faithful and to delight in friendships with others who are faithful and truthful.
I want to truly delight in you;
I want the desires in my heart to be the same as the desires in yours, Lord. Your delight, your joy.

Sometimes I will write the Psalm patterned prayer out in a notebook; other times, I just pray through it, as I read the passage over several times. Over time, I have discovered that it seems most effective to actually journal my own words that are patterned after the psalm.

I believe we will find this method to be incredibly refreshing and encouraging. Praying through the Psalms in this way brings the gift of God's perspective. It is also a great feeling to know that the ancient greats of the faith prayed these same psalms. David prayed many of these psalms, as did the early members of the ancient synagogues and the early church. We may find great comfort, as well as a sense of connection to God, by praying along the same themes that God's people have been praying for the past thousands of years.

Through using this method of praying the Psalms, or praying the scriptures, we will come to realize that all the words of the Bible are inspired by God, they are God-breathed. (2 Timothy 3:16) Likewise, human breath is also God-breathed, for God breathed the breath into Adam (Genesis 2:7). It is no wonder then, that we may experience great comfort when we breathed out, or when we speak out, the very inspired words of God within our own prayers. We may became comforted knowing that these same words brought comfort to David, to Solomon, to the prophets, to the early Christians, and to Jesus himself. For me, I found that nothing seems to be able to calm me like praying out the Psalms does. I also use this method to pray the Psalms at times when I just don't know what to pray for, and sometimes during those times when I just don't feel like praying. At those times, we don't even have to think about *what* to pray, for the prayers are already written. We merely allow the written prayers of the Psalms to inspire our own words, and each time we will be refreshed by His words.

Now, to be clear, I did not start at Psalms 1 and pray through all of the psalms verse by verse. To do so would not have been inspiring – it would have felt like an assignment, like required homework. We will discover, as we read read through the Psalms, that some of the passages are dark and depressing. So for the most part, I would read through, and oftentimes I would skim through the Psalms, until I found a passage that seemed to connect with me, a passage that would seem to "jump out" at me and make me think, "I want to pray that!"

For another example, on another day, I was skimming through the Psalms, until I reached Psalm 69. In the first part of Psalm 69, David is lamenting over how it seems thousands or even millions of people hate him and are out to destroy him. Thankfully, I haven't personally related to such a perilous experience, so I kept reading until I came to verse 14; and then I read this:

Deliver me from sinking in the mire;
let me be delivered from my enemies and from the deep waters.
Let not the flood sweep over me,
or the deep swallow me up,
or the pit close its mouth over me.

Answer me, O Lord, for your steadfast love is good;
according to your abundant mercy, turn to me.
Hide not your face from your servant;
for I am in distress; make haste to answer me.
Draw near to my soul....

I thought about those verses above, and I pondered them briefly, and then I wrote out the following prayer. Then I prayed out the prayer based on the same pattern, the same themes, but in my own words –

"Lord, I ask you to go before me because you know what problems and difficulties I will face. I ask you to rescue me

and deliver me from any troubles or difficulties that lie ahead. I ask you that, if there is anyone in my life who is being dishonest with me – I ask you to reveal it to me and deliver me from any snares they may be setting up for me.

Oh God, I do not know what troubles tomorrow or the future may bring, but I pray that the floods of life, and the deep pits of troubles and disappointment do not overcome me. I pray for you to go before me and to reduce or prevent any troubles and difficulties that I may have to face soon.

God – your love is so good. I know you will answer me; and I pray that you answer me based on your mercy. I want to know you, to experience you. Please do not hide yourself from me. When I pray, please answer me quickly. I want nothing more than to draw near to you. Please draw near to my soul, Lord."

I have one one more example to give. This time, I picked pick up where I left off at Psalm 69:18, and I continued reading until I came to another passage that motivated me to pray it in my own words. I read until Psalm 71:17. When I came to these verses, I found that I immediately identified with the words, and I wanted to pray these words as David did. So I turned the passage into a prayer, once again. Here are the words from the Psalms:

*O God, from my youth you have taught me,
and I still proclaim your wondrous deeds.
So even to old age and gray hairs,
O God, do not forsake me,
until I proclaim your might to another generation,
your power to all those who come.*

And these were the my words of prayer, patterned by the verses above:

"O God, I have learned about you, and learned from you, since I was a young child.
Out of all the things I learned as a child and in school, you are the most wondrous, and I continue to love you and proclaim you.
I pray Lord, that the closeness that I feel with you will remain with me – even until old age when every hair on my head is gray;

Do not let this closeness leave; do not leave me. Keep me from distractions and obstacles that would allow me to slip into a pattern of distance from You.

Oh Lord, I hope to have a role in proclaiming you to the next generation,
my desire for my life is to live a life that demonstrates you, your goodness and trustworthiness, and your power – and I pray that something I do leaves a mark that touches and inspires members of the next generation to know you as I have known you – and even to know you better and more closely than I have known you."

So finally, to conclude and summarize the second simple method for praying or journaling the Psalms, here are the recommended steps:

1. Start reading through/skimming through the Psalms. Either start at the beginning or skim and read until a passage is found which causes you to be motivated to pray its pattern or its themes. Also, there are some

suggested passages in the *Resources* section at the end of this book to help you get started.
2. Read the particular passage you have chosen closely and think about re-writing the words in your own words and in your current situation.
3. Write, speak, or pray out the passage in your own words, putting yourself in the perspective of the psalmist, yet in the present time.
4. Write down your Psalm inspired prayer in your own words in your prayer journal, along with the date that you wrote it.

4
A Simple Effective Method of Prayer #3
Praying with Journaling

I think that this chapter, and this method, could be the most important of all for walking close with God. In fact, at first, I wanted to write an entire book about journaling alone.

Here is another mystery that I hope you will apply and discover: Journaling your prayer requests will change your life, grow your faith to unshakeable levels, and prepare you for spiritual breakthroughs in your walk with God.

Would you like to grow your faith to unshakeable levels and start experiencing spiritual breakthroughs in your level of trust in God? If so, then start journaling your prayers. I actually try to refrain from becoming "too preachy" in my writing, but I have to explain that prayer journaling is something I am emphatic about.

Start journaling and keep journaling. Start this week. Start today.

When we keep track of our prayer requests – all of them, large and small – we are able to watch and record how God uses our prayers, over time, to weave our life together. It is beautiful, to say the least. It is confidence and faith building, to say more.

You will want to write down your prayer requests, and you

will also want to write down any insights you believe you receive during your prayer time, anything that God prompts you to do.

Two of the main practical reasons that I keep a journal are these:

1) I do not want to forget what I have prayed for, and
2) I do not want to forget all that the Lord has done for me!

So get a notebook or a journal, and each day write down your prayer requests and write the date of the prayer.

Do this even for the little prayer requests; do this <u>especially</u> for the little prayer requests!

Why bother writing down the small prayer requests? We do this because, when we are lifting up prayers over small things all the time, we likely won't even remember half of what we have prayed for. At least I don't remember all of the "little things" I pray about. So at least once or twice a week, I sit down and quickly write down things I have prayed about, and I put the date next to them. The following week, I will look at the prior weeks' lists and then make a note and mark the date if the prayer request was answered. From this exercise, I have seen that God really does hear and answer every prayer – little or big – in time. Even better, He never stops receiving and responding to prayer. Week after week, year after year, your prayer journal will demonstrate to you, without doubt, that when you draw near to God, He draws near to you. Every time.

I became so amazed to see all the little prayers I had prayed, and to see the received answers. Furthermore, if I hadn't tracked those little prayer requests, I likely would never have even realized that most of them had been answered. I would have completely forgotten that I prayed for that small thing in the first place.

Without my prayer journal, the Lord would still have been working in my life. I want to clarify that I am not saying that keeping a prayer journal causes God to act in any way. God is acting on our prayer; however, we often don't even notice what He has done for us! When we don't notice, we don't build our faith. We start to grow lukewarm in our faith and trust in God.

Here is an example of one little thing I prayed about just one time. My oldest daughter went through a period, lasting over a year, in which she had a very sour attitude about school and learning. She hated math (even though she is quite good at it); she rushed through her work; she wrote short two to three sentence paragraphs for her essays, even though she was capable of writing an exquisite composition if she would just apply herself. One day, I prayed about this, and in my journal, I simply wrote this: "please help my daughter to change her attitude towards her schoolwork, and please let me know if there is something I should be doing to help her with that." I prayed this little prayer just one time. I didn't dwell on it at all. I didn't keep praying about the situation over and over. I actually wasn't overly worried or burdened by her attitude, because as a former teacher, I was aware that many middle school students go through a period of having a negative attitude towards schoolwork. I prayed this little prayer about my daughter just one time. Afterwards, I completely forgot that I even prayed about it.

Then, about two or three weeks later, as I was preparing dinner one evening, my daughter waltzed into the kitchen and said, "Mom, I've decided that I am going to take my schoolwork more seriously and do my best. I want to be proud of my work; and I want to start building good habits for high school and college." I was busy with dinner, and I hardly paid her any attention. I responded with something like, "Hmmm, okay that's a great decision." Then my daughter waltzed right out of the room just as she came in. No further conversation took place. The very next day, I did notice that she did start displaying more motivation and effort in her school work.

However, I had completely forgotten that I had even prayed about her attitude towards school. I had prayed about it only one time, weeks prior to this announcement in the kitchen. Another week passed, and I took some time one evening to review the prayer requests I had written in my journal. That was when I saw that on March 18th, I had prayed that God would help her improve her attitude towards her schoolwork. On April 8th, I was able to write down that my little prayer had been answered. I was so excited to realize that this prayer had been answered so clearly, especially since I honestly had completely forgotten I had even prayed about it!

Afterwards, I talked to my daughter about what happened to improve her attitude towards school. She told me that she had participated in a conversation with my mother, her grandmother. The conversation took place the same day she waltzed into the kitchen, announcing her improved attitude and focus. During that conversation, something that her grandmother said inspired my daughter to completely change her attitude. This increased my faith and trust even more in the Lord's response to prayer. When prayers are answered like this, I know that I can give my problems – any problem, big or small – to God and he will find a way to weave a response in my life. In this case, he didn't even use me to solve it! He used my prayer and my mother! She somehow was prompted to be the motivating influence for my daughter, and I didn't even know what was happening! And to think, if I hadn't been journaling I would have completely forgotten that I had prayed this. I would have missed this small but incredibly special answer to prayer. I would have missed what God had done for me and my family.

How many times do we miss, or do we not even realize, what God is doing or has done for us – because we don't write down and track little prayers? I believe we miss a lot. I know we miss a lot. In fact, I don't know anyone who has kept a prayer journal and has announced that it did not increase their faith and trust in the Lord. Journaling is a faith building activity. It will increase your faith to unshakeable limits.

Since then, there have been numerous times that I have jotted down small little prayers, the types of little prayers that are so small and seem so insignificant that I only pray them one time. Then I jot it down, and then go on with life. If I hadn't written it down, I would have forgotten I even prayed for these small things.

Instead, I now know that God answers every prayer. You can know this too, by keeping your own prayer journal.

In my life, God used....
a little prayer of little faith...

and a little talk between a grandma and her granddaughter…
to weave a testimony of something He did for us…
and I am able to now share that small testimony with you, to encourage you in your own prayer life.

Isn't that what is amazing also! Now these tiny, seemingly insignificant prayer requests become testimonies to the work of God in your life. Your answers to prayer from your journal will build your faith, and if you ever share some of them with others, you will be able to help others build their faith.

That is how God uses small situations, plus faith as a mustard seed for His glory. However, let's repeat it again: *It doesn't do any good if you don't remember what you prayed for, nor remember what He has done!* If you don't remember, it doesn't build your faith. If you don't remember, you can't tell others. This is why journaling isn't just a good idea – it's a necessity in the life of a believer pursuing the best of what God has to give.

No other activity helped me to explain to my children why I was able to have so much faith and trust in God. When you keep a prayer journal, if you have children or grandchildren, you can sit down with them and show and tell them: "Look I prayed for this on March 12 and here, on May 5th, that prayer was answered!" I could also show them how time after time, each prayer had been answered. I can also show them that sometimes I prayed for something, and God answered later with a "no." I could explain to them that because God answered so many prayers positively, that I could still trust that His "no" is for the best. It became so exciting to realize that we were literally tracking the work of God's spirit in our lives. What a faith building activity this was to do!

Now, before we close this chapter and start thinking that the prayer journal method works like a "magic genie," I have to warn us that we must keep reading. Because the prayer journal method of tracking prayers is not a "method" nor a formula which will force God into quickly answering your prayers. It is not a method to be used to test the Lord. There is more to it, and this leads us to the harder part of prayer and prayer journaling.

The Harder Part of Prayer Tracking

This is the section of this book that I cannot just tiptoe around or leave out. It will probably be the most straightforward portion of the book. This is the hardest part of our communion with God. It is the hardest part of our relationship with Him.

As we pray, and as we grow closer to God, He will place something in our hearts that He wants us to follow through on. Most likely, God, through the Holy Spirit, will convict us that we need to change a habit, an attitude, or a behavior. (John 16:8)

Prayer is most effective when it is prayed by a person who is eagerly choosing to follow God's prompting and His leading, especially with regards to these personal convictions that are received in prayer.

Prayer tracking in a journal will become more than just tracking your own requests to God. As you pray earnestly;

as you spend more focused time in prayer, you will, at times, receive clear conviction of actions you need to cease, or behaviors you need to change. This is the process of sanctification. When God places such a conviction on you; He is doing so because He is inviting you to come closer to Him.

What is this like? You may wonder, "How can I know what the Lord is convicting me to do?"

I can share my personal testimony in an attempt to explain. I can only tell you what my experience has been; and I have confirmed with other Christians who have experienced conviction during the sanctification process in the same way.

A person who has been in relationship with the Spirit of the Lord is able to differentiate their own thoughts from the Lord's instruction to them. I can tell you that my own experience may be described like this: my own thoughts come from my brain and they are fleeting and easily changed. When the human brain is working, it effects the muscles of the eyes, and I can also feel these eye sensations and know that it is just my own thoughts. However, when the Lord gives me a conviction, it comes in the form of a feeling of pressure in my chest, right above my heart. My eye muscles are not affected. The Bible tells us that the word of the Lord pierces the spirit and discerns the thoughts of the heart (Hebrews 4:12). It is difficult to describe; but a message from the Lord is a conviction that is clear and firm. In other words, the message is convicting, and I know in my spirit that it is a true, unchanging message – the message does not change when it comes from the Lord.

Also, if I don't obey the conviction from God; it doesn't just go away. I may be able to ignore it for a while, even for years I may be able to ignore it, but it will keep coming back to me. I won't be able to "shake it off."

Sometimes, especially early in the process of growing closer to God, the message will be to stop doing something that we know from the Bible is clearly a sin. For example, we may be convicted to stop drinking excessively, to stop gossiping, or to stop entertaining sinful thoughts.

This is just the first step of sanctification. At first, early in our walk to continued closeness with God, He will convict us that we need to stop doing things that He has already clearly told us about in His word. These are the behaviors or thoughts that you are repeating or harboring that are in clear contradiction to His word. These are behaviors, thoughts, or attitudes that are sinful for all of His people – so clearly so that He documented these behaviors through His spirit, through men and prophets, in the Bible. These are sins or behaviors which will block anyone, including you, from being as close as possible to the Spirit of God. These are sins that will clearly block your prayer life, will clog up your line of communication with God, and *may* even delay your ability to receive consistent help and blessings from Him.

However, the personal process of sanctification does not stop with those things we are told to cease doing from the Bible. The sins mentioned in the Bible are sinful for all people, and these you will be convicted of first. *However, when you obey that which is clearly stated by God in the Bible; then a next level of personal sanctification will likely begin.*

Do you remember the story of the rich young ruler who came to Jesus? It is found in Matthew 19. The wealthy man came to Jesus and asked, "What good thing do I need to do to have eternal life?" Jesus replied that he should keep the commandments, including, "You shall not commit murder; you shall not commit adultery; you shall not steal; you shall not bear false witness; honor your mother and father; and you shall love your neighbor as yourself." The wealthy, young ruler, replied, *"I have done all of these things; what am I lacking?"* And Jesus replied, "If you want to be complete, sell all your possessions and give to the poor, and you will have treasure in Heaven; and come, follow me."

In this story, Jesus first reminds the rich ruler of the basic, important commandments which were already in the law. By doing so; he convicts the man of what he has already been taught in the word of God. *Next, after the man claims that he has already kept these commandments; Jesus convicts the man of something personal – something that likely only applies to this man and his circumstances. I have found that we are still convicted by the Spirit in a similar two-step manner today.*

Is it conviction or inspiration?
Before I continue, I need to make a clear statement so as not to cause confusion: *The conviction of sanctification is different from feelings of inspiration.* You may feel *inspired* to start a large ministry. That does not mean you should quit your job and do so, *just because you are inspired.* Conviction is different – it is not an exciting idea, nor a general feeling of motivation to go in a certain

direction. It's not merely a desire to start something new. It is not merely a dream or a goal you feel inspired to reach. *A conviction from the Lord is piercing. It is certain, firm, unwaverable.* You will *know* that it is what God wants. *If you have to question yourself whether or not God is really convicting you to take a certain action or to change direction – then it probably is not a conviction.* Continue to pray through, using the methods described in this book; but do not make major life changes unless you are certain it is a conviction. Talking to a trusted and experienced pastor or minister may be helpful if you are not sure if what you are experiencing is a conviction or just inspiration.

So again, once you obey those clear messages that are biblically based; you may then start receiving personal convictions to change your ways – even though your current ways may not be clearly sinful. For example, once I had a small home business in which I was marketing and selling a nutritional product to others. It was a "side-business;" that earned some extra income for our family. However, I began to be convicted in my prayer time that I was to close that business because it was taking up too much of my time; and God had another plan for how He wanted me to use my time. This message was confusing for me. I had no doubt that God wanted me to stop the business. But why would it matter, I thought? Certainly it isn't a sin. There is no command in the Bible to "do not sell wares on the side to earn extra income for your family." In fact, the Proverbs 31 woman is blessed because she sees opportunities, right?

So I did not obey the conviction. Yet the conviction kept returning. After about a full year had passed, I still did not close down the business, but I did scale back on the time I spent on it; and I only provided products for existing customers and stopped marketing for new customers. Even so, the conviction continued clearly in my heart, that I was to completely close the business. Eventually, after more than two years had passed since I was first convicted; I did close the business and completely stopped selling the nutritional product.

I realized that even though there was nothing clearly Biblically wrong with my business, that the conviction from God was clearly telling me to stop spending my extra time on it. *Even though having such a business may not be wrong for others; it was wrong for me to continue after God convicted me it was time to close.* As I struggled with God, He finally let me know that the business was taking up too much of my available time; and that He wanted to use that time for something else. At the time I finally obeyed; I did not know what that "something else" was. Shortly after I obeyed His conviction, God convicted me again – to start writing about Him. He wanted me to study and write about what His Son Jesus had taught us; and He wanted me to write about my own journey in drawing near to Him. Within a year of closing the business, I published my first book with God leading and convicting me all along the way.

Along this journey of writing; God has continued to convict me; and now, it is easier to follow through in obedience without waiting and floundering for a year or two. There have been temptations along the way in my writing journey – too. For example, since I was a young girl I have always enjoyed reading and writing. My genre of choice is mystery fiction. The truth is, I really, really want to write a mystery book. I also have the temptation of hearing from many writing colleagues who tell me over and over that the fiction market is a bigger market than the non-fiction market; and that if I write a mystery book I will make more money in less time that I can ever earn from publishing non-fiction books.

The truth is – I really want to write a mystery book. However, God has clearly convicted me that I am to write books that will help Christians stay closer to Him, that will inspire and help others to walk closer with Him.

I even tried to figure out a way I could write a mystery book that is also a Christian book that would help God's people stay closer to Him. I prayed about that, but again God clearly let me know through that pressure of conviction in my heart that no, it's not fiction for me to write at this time.

So here I am following God's conviction on my heart – writing this very book you are reading – not because it is the book I want to write, but because it is the book I believe God wants me to write. God hasn't promised me any fame or fortune; He hasn't promised me a bestseller by any means. He convicted me that I am to write, even if it only helps just a handful of other people walk closer to Him. I am to write for the spiritual blessings it may bring....not for earthly blessings. I am to focus on His unseen promises, and not on the things I can see.

And that, my reader, is my very personal example of the process of sanctification. God took me first, from repenting of those clear sins. Then He took me from wanting to spend my free time from doing things of my own choice, to convicting me and motivating me to using my free time to do something for Him. When I obey those convictions – He draws closer; and we continue the "trust walk;" and He never leaves; and so far, He always has a new conviction sometime after I have obeyed the last one.

I write my own personal example above, certainly not as a way to boast about myself. The truth is this: yes, I did finally obey God; but I did not obey Him quickly, whatsoever. I share this story not to boast by any means. If anything, I find this story shameful to share because I admit I did not obey God right away. *I share this story because I believe that some of the readers of this book are in the same situation right now.* God has placed a pressure point of conviction in your heart, convicting you that there is something in your life you need to either stop doing or start doing. His conviction for you is not related to a clear sin spelled out from the Bible. *But God wants you to stop doing that activity because He has better plans for your time.* He has His plans for your time; and He is not going to clearly reveal His better plans to you until you obey His first conviction He has given you. It is revealed step by step. Obey Him in the first thing; and only then will He unfold His plan for you for the better thing to take place.

So after explaining all of that – let's get back to how this relates to prayer journaling. While you will use your prayer journal to write down your requests to God; *you will also use it to write down those things God convicts you to do, or to stop doing.*

A few thoughts:

Prayer without confession is not incredibly effective. So

always include confession as part of your prayer.

Secondly, distracted prayer is not particularly effective, so use the methods given in this book, as well as your prayer journal, to keep focused in prayer.

Finally, a convicted heart that has not obeyed may be less effective in prayer. This is the hardest part of prayer journaling – writing down what God convicts you to do. Pray over it and follow through.

Remember again, that conviction is different from inspiration. This clarification is worth repeating in full so that readers of this book are not confused on this point. You may feel inspired to start a large ministry. That does not mean you should quit your job and do so, just because you are inspired. Conviction is different – it is not an exciting idea, or a uncertain motivation to go in a certain direction. It's not merely a desire to start something new. It is not merely a dream or a goal you feel inspired to reach. A conviction from the Lord is piercing. It is certain, firm, unwaverable. You will *know* that it is what God wants. *If you have to question yourself whether or not God is really convicting you to take a certain action or to change direction – then it probably is not a conviction.* Continue to pray through, using the methods described in this book; but do not make major life changes unless you are certain it is a conviction. Talking to a trusted and experienced pastor or minister may be helpful if you are not sure if what you are experiencing is a conviction or just inspiration.

To conclude this chapter, let's remember that this chapter overall, is about journaling your prayer requests, and also journaling convictions that you receive from God. The summary action steps for this method are:

1) Begin writing your prayer requests to God, including even the "little prayer requests." Write the date of the prayer request too.
2) Review your prayer requests at least once a week and make a note when they are answered. Also write the date when they are answered.
3) Also, write down any convictions you receive from the Lord. Also write the date of when the conviction was given; and then write the date that you followed through.
4) Keep your journal as evidence of the Lord's working in your life; evidence of His response to every prayer; and evidence that He convicts and also leads you in His will. No practice will increase your faith more than keeping a record of all that God has done and is doing for you.

5

A Simple Effective Method of Prayer #4
Keeping God in Mind, through Jesus

What are some of the promises of God you can think of off the top of your head? I know some of the first examples that come to my mind are ones like these:

the promise of peace over anxiety,

the promise to give us wisdom,

and the promises to guide us in the way we should go.

Yet there is one very basic promise that God absolutely guarantees to those of us who seek Him. It is a promise that is so obvious, that we often merely overlook it. When I remind you of this very basic promise, your first response may be to think -- "Oh yeah. I know that. I've known that a long time. Yes, that is very basic. Even a 5 year old child learns it in church. Certainly you must have something better in your theology that that to share with us today."

One of the *most basic, yet greatest* promises of God to all His people is this:

He is near....
and He hears.

When you fully grasp the truth that God's *is near* and that God *desires to hear from you,*

When you grasp the **understanding of His** *nearness* and *availability, and you allow that knowledge to* sink deep into your heart and mind --

You will never be able to get over what happens from that point forward in your life. Your life will be forever changed if you keep that truth front and center each day and throughout the day. Your perceptions will be transformed to be more like His. Your thoughts will be transformed to be more like His. Your decision making will be transformed. Your emotions will be transformed. Your heart will be transformed.

A few years ago, I came to realize that I was so busy and scheduled each day, that I didn't take hardly any time to even think about God -- except maybe in my devotional time and in a quick prayer time before I fell asleep at night. In effect, I thought about God some at the beginning and at the end of the day; but not much at all throughout the day. It was as if I merely checked in with God in the morning and checked out at night.

And during this time (I remember specifically it was January, 2013), a number of "30 day challenges" were being promoted. I would see ads and promotions for "take this 30 day weight loss challenge;" or "take this 30 day fitness challenge." Even the church had some challenges to encourage us: "take the 30 day Bible reading challenge," or "take a 30 day memory verse challenge."

At the beginning of that month, and at the beginning of that year, the Spirit deeply pressed a conviction on my heart. I realized that I needed to participate in a challenge too; but the challenge I would participate in would be very personal. I had been both curious and perplexed about one of the largest challenges the Bible gives to us -- one that seems impossible. See, the Bible, challenges us to love the Lord with all our heart, soul, and mind. And it goes even further than that by telling us to pray continually.

So the Biblical challenge is this: keep all your mind on the Lord all the time.

I wondered -- *can anyone do such a thing*? Then I wondered, why would the Bible tell us to do something if it wasn't possible? Next I wondered, *how* could someone do such a thing? Or at least, how could someone *try* to do such a thing?

And then a very simple, very childlike idea came to me. Using a child-level idea, I set up a private challenge for myself. I created a personal plan of action that some of you may think is silly. I decided that, for me, the only way I could come close to keeping the Lord on my mind all day would be to pretend that He was actually physically with me, as well as being spiritually with me.

I'm actually a little embarrassed to tell the lengths I had to go to in order to attempt to keep the Lord on my mind. Again, because it seems so simple, so childlike, and even maybe a little immature. Yet, do you know who else did what I am about to describe to you? King David. David seemed to have taken a personal "think about God as much as possible" challenge throughout his life. Yet David wasn't too embarrassed to tell about it. He wrote all about his walking with the Lord and talking with the Lord, all throughout his life. Here is what we find in some of David's psalms:

" I know the LORD is always with me. I will not be shaken, for he is right beside me."
Psalm 18:8 (ESV)

"But as for me, the nearness of God is my good;
I have made the Lord GOD my refuge,
That I may tell of all Your works.
Psalm 73:38 (ESV)
"The LORD is near to all who call upon Him, To all who call upon Him in truth."
Psalm 145:18 (ESV)

So here it is: I decided to take a "Remember He is With You Challenge" for 30 days straight.

During these 30 days, I would remember that God was with me *all the time* by pretending, like a child pretends in his imagination, that He was actually physically with me.

See, I would wake up in the morning and think of Jesus as if He was sitting at the foot of my bed, saying "Good morning! This is a new day God has for you." Then He would follow me into the bathroom -- yes even the bathroom -- and sit on the edge of the tub as I brushed my teeth. There, He would help me get my thoughts ready for the day.

Next, I would leave to drive to work, and He would sit in the passenger seat of my car, and we would talk about whatever was on my mind for the day. He would lead me to think about the challenges that might come up at work that day, and He would cause me to consider how to best approach handling them.

While at work, I would be extremely busy, of course. So, I decided to put an extra empty chair in one of the corners of my office, and to me, that was "His chair." Whenever I would get a few minutes break from working on a written report, I would imagine He was there. Although I was really busy, that chair reminded me that if something stressful happened during the day, I could immediately consider Him for help. If I had a stressful meeting, I would just imagine Jesus sitting right there physically in the room, at an empty seat at the conference table, watching over everything, and reminding me -- *I will guide you through your troubles, so please remember I am here, and I want you to genuinely depend on me.*

Finally, on the drive home from work, I would pretend Jesus would be physically in my passenger seat again, reminding me that even though my day had been long and tiring, that I should remember to have patience with the children, and all the household tasks, and all the after-school tasks that keep us busy. At home, He had a place on the sofa in the living room; and He would help me to remain calm when the children started fighting or in whatever happened or needed to be done while with my family.

I did this all in my own mind. Even my husband and my children didn't know I was doing this. Of course I didn't tell them. I couldn't let them know my mind was so weak that I had to play child-like imagination games with myself, in order to remember God.

Well, let me tell you what happened. I scheduled and followed this personal "Remember He is with You" challenge for 30 days straight.

Simply put -- it was a very enjoyable month, and by about day 20, I didn't have to "pretend" anymore that He was there.

I no longer had to pretend on His presence; because by that time, I could perceive His presence. After only 20 days or so, I couldn't get Him or His ways out of mind if I tried. Finally, finally! I had found His presence.

And it changed my life, *again*, in words I cannot even begin to describe. I had called myself a Christian for over 30 years, but it changed me and took me to a new level of intimacy with God all over again. Following through with this challenge brought so many things into perspective during that time. It helped me to discern and make better decisions. It enabled me to quickly prioritize. It helped me to keep my cool, calm my anxieties, and to truly look forward to a great day --

a great day no matter what!

And how could I know it would be a great day no matter what?

I could know this because I could truly claim a genuine promise of God -- the promise that He is *NEAR* and He will *HEAR* !

Why, oh why, is this simple truth so hard for so many of us to keep at the forefront of our thinking each day, throughout the day?

So what do you think I am going to do next?

Well, of course, I am going to pass this challenge along to you. *Now I want to challenge some of you to take this "silly, childlike challenge" to remember God is with you as much as you can every day, for 30 days straight.*

Start today, and for the next 30 days, remember as much as you can -- all day long -- that He is near. God is near. Christ's spirit is near. Keep that thought in your mind and meditate on it as often as you can.

And if that is hard for you to do (like it was for me) -- then maybe my simple, childlike practice will help you, just like it did for me. Just pretend Jesus is right there with you, all day long. Just like a child would do. Imagine he is sitting next to you in the car. Imagine that He has a chair in your living room or your office. When you leave, He will go with you, even walking alongside you. Then He finds a new place to sit in the next room, building, vehicle, or area where you are. As you walk down the hall, He walks with you. And all throughout the day, He is guiding you, calming you, helping you, and advising you.

So take this 30 day challenge this month! I dare you to do it!

Some of the *best promises* you may claim from God -- the promises *that will make the greatest difference in your life for the better* -- are those promises *that are actually the most basic* and *simple truths about God's very own nature.*

The promises of his nearness and his desire to hear from you are, in my opinion, the most basic promises He guarantees us. "We are confident that God listens to us if we ask for anything that has his approval." - 1 John 5:14 (GOD'S WORD translation)

6
Motivation to Pray

"...the Spirit pleads for us believers in harmony with God's own will."
Romans 8:27b

A number of Christians from various denominations may be asked, "What are some reasons that may cause you to go a day or longer without praying?" They may also be asked, "Why don't you pray more often?"

These are some reasons that are often given:

I just was too busy today.
I usually pray in the morning; and I overslept. I intended to pray later in the day, but then I forgot to do so, because praying later isn't my usual routine.
I prayed in bed before going to sleep; and I fell asleep during the prayer. So I 'half-prayed.'
There really aren't any major problems or obstacles I have right now, so I don't feel the need to pray.
I don't need to bother God with my little concerns when there are much bigger concerns and problems in the world.
God already knows what is going to happen and what He is going to do. I don't think prayer is going to make a difference.

Do you ever use any of these excuses to validate reasons for not spending time in formal prayer? To all of those excuses, I respond to you with this question:

Do you truly understand what happens when you pray? What do you think actually happens when you pray? Take a minute and answer that question for yourself.

Here are a few things from the Bible that tell us what actually happens when you pray to God:

You receive from Him. You open yourself up to what He has for you. You also receive what you ask of Him, in His timing, if what you ask is in accordance to His will. Matthew 7:7-8

Your prayer messages and requests literally raise up to the heavens, like a sweet smelling incense (Revelation 5:8). In other words, your prayers do reach the spirits of Heaven, they are received. Your prayers are heard by the Holy one and His heavenly angels.

Your prayers may empower and enable the angels to intercede for you (example in Daniel 10:12-14).

Your prayers connect you to the spirit of the Lord; your prayers allow your spiritual eyes and ears to be opened, in order to give you wisdom (Psalms 119:18; Ephesians 1:18).

Even if you don't know what to pray, the Holy Spirit will intercede for you and pray for you on your behalf. (Romans 8:26)

I don't know about you, but when I look over that list of what prayer actually accomplishes, I would be afraid to start a day off without prayer, without receiving wisdom from God, without having the Holy Spirit to intercede for me on things I do not even know to expect or to pray for! A day without prayer is like stepping onto a spiritual battlefield with absolutely no protection and no strategy for protecting yourself nor for being victorious. Just as you wouldn't leave your house in the morning without the proper shoes to protect your feet; don't leave the home without your prayers, your spiritual protection.

The armor of God is worn through prayer. (Ephesians 6:10-18)
The wisdom and guidance of God is received through prayer. (James 1:5)
The protection of God is received through prayer. Even protection for troubles you don't know about which will face in the future! (Matthew 6:3)
The intercession of the Holy Spirit is gained through prayer! (Romans 8:26)

When we truly ponder all that prayer accomplishes in our lives; we have to ask ourselves why would we ever skip a day, or even an hour, without prayer?

Here are some questions to ponder:

What is usually the most important issue on your mind each day?

What is the most important event or item on your mind today?

Is it keeping an appointment? Making sure you complete the priority item on your "to do" list?

Is it keeping track of your personal and family schedule?

Are you keeping a running mental list of what needs to be done for work?

Perhaps you are mentally problem solving various scenarios at work, at home, or in your relationships?

All of the types of concerns listed above take priority in our lives. They fill our minds and our calendars. Furthermore, if you have an appointment, you know you have to make it or go through a possible hassle to have to reschedule. If you have a deadline at work, you must make that deadline or there could be consequences, such as a poor work review or even a loss of your job! If you have a hectic family and personal schedule, you know that there are certain times of the day that certain things must happen. For example, you must drop your children off at school and then pick them up each day at a certain time, or else there will be consequences for your children as well as for yourself.

All of these examples are appointments, deadlines, and schedules that we meet and keep at the forefront of our minds through the day. If we are the more forgetful type, we likely keep a calendar of some sort, whether it be on paper or on Outlook. Sometimes, when I have an important yet not regularly scheduled appointment, I will even set an alarm reminder on my smart phone so that when the alarm goes off, I remember that it is time to leave for the appointment.

One reason these types of appointments and errands are priorities in days is due to the very fact *that there can be major negative consequences if we don't make these events and issues a priority in our lives.* Missing physical appointments and personal deadlines means missing the benefits that go along with meeting those appointments and deadlines. Maintaining those appointments and deadlines means maintaining the benefits and any desired outcomes that may be earned from simply doing what you are scheduled or planned to do.

So friends, let's stop and consider the benefits and consequences of prayer and spiritual appointments. Has anyone ever truly explained to you the benefits that are received into your life when you make and keep appointments with God? Keeping the spiritual appointments means maintaining the benefits. Not keeping the spiritual appointments means the benefits may not be obtained.

So what is the difference? Does it matter?

Let's look at the list from the opening of this chapter and look at it from the opposite vantage point. **What do we miss out on when we do not pray?**

When we do not pray....

We do not receive from Him. We do not spiritually open ourselves to receive what He has for us.

When we do not pray...

We do not send any messages or requests up to the heavens. I believe our messages go up to the heavens like the sweet smelling incense described in Revelation. Simply put, if we do not pray, we are not heard.

When we do not pray….

We are not walking in connection with the Spirit of the Lord; our spiritual eyes and ears are not opened to important moments in the day; we are not able to readily receive the wisdom He has to guide us throughout the day.

When we do not pray….

We do not activate the Holy Spirit's intercession for us. Sometimes we think that everything is fine and that we don't think we need to pray for anything specific. Yet, the Holy Spirit knows what is in our near future, and knows what is laying around the corner for us. *The Spirit intercedes for us and on our behalf on issues and events and troubles that wait for us in our future! However, we miss out on this when we do not pray.*

I don't know about you, but when I look over that list of what prayer actually accomplishes, I would be afraid to start a day off without prayer, without receiving wisdom from God, without having the Holy Spirit to intercede for me on things I do not even know to expect or to pray for! A day without prayer is like stepping onto a spiritual battlefield with absolutely no protection and no strategy for protecting ourselves. Just as you wouldn't leave your house in the morning without the proper shoes to protect your feet; don't leave the home without your prayers, your spiritual protection.

Let's keep going….when we do not pray…

We do not wear the armor of God; meaning we do not

have assurance of His protection. We may not receive protection from future events that we don't even know we will be facing.

We do not readily receive the wisdom and guidance that God has for us. God reveals His wisdom to us step by step, over time. If we are not in regular prayer, we do not receive his next "dose" of wisdom that we may sorely need.

We may not gain the benefit of having the Holy Spirit intercede for us, directing our paths throughout and around future troubles we don't even know will exist. This is a huge benefit in our lives! Let us not let this powerful gift go dormant in our lives!

Do you have a time appointed for prayer each and every day? If so, this book has hopefully helped you to more fully understand how that prayer appointment in shaping your life. Hopefully you are motivated to continue in the regular practice of prayer, and to also take you into a deeper understanding of what prayer is and how to pray more authentically in a manner to draw closer to God.

On the other hand, if you do not have a prayer appointment on your current personal daily schedule, then realize that, just as there are significant consequences for missing in-person appointments and daily deadlines, *there are even greater consequences for missing prayer appointments*. However, we typically don't even realize what we are missing out on. Going through life without regular prayer appointments and time with God is like choosing to live in a mundane, monotonous, day to day life. Making and keeping prayer appointments and spending time with God is choosing to fill your life with purpose, protection, assurance, and anticipation of what He will do.

In the physical world, there are very clear and oftentimes immediate consequences for missing regularly scheduled appointments and deadlines. If you miss your annual checkups with the doctor, you could be developing a disease without knowing it; and by the time you are finally diagnosed, the condition may be much worse than it could have been had you kept your regular appointments. Likewise, in the spiritual world, the consequences for missing appointments with God are just as great; *however, because we do not have our minds tuned in to the patterns of God's ways and the patterns of the spiritual – we don't always identify the consequence as being related to our string of missed prayer appointments with God.*

I hope that as we near the end of this little book, that we will realize that our prayer appointments and time spent with God are the most important appointments of our day. I hope we will realize that **the Lord has made many promises to those who draw near to Him; and the consequence of not drawing near to Him means you are likely missing out on those promises!**

The promises received through prayer are not always immediately seen; and because they are not easily quantifiable, we often don't even realize what we are missing out on, until it is too late and we have fallen into a state of spiritual apathy and dormancy. When this happens, we are prone to attacks of the mind in which we may blame ourselves or blame others for any misfortunes we encounter. We do not realize that our apathetic state has developed because we were not keeping our appointments with God. We do not realize the great value we have missed, spiritual value and benefits that accumulate and accelerate like spiritual compound interest over the years.

Just consider – what will your life look life if you are regularly making authentic, daily spiritual prayer deposits into your soul? How might those benefits accumulate and accelerate over time? What might next year be like in your life and your relationships? What may it look like in five years? In ten years? At the end of your life? What may it look like when you are ushered into the presence of heaven and finally are reunited with the One who you have been spiritually meeting with every single day?

So what is it that seems to be first and foremost in our thinking each day? What one thing are you concentrating on above everything else on any given day? What is the priority of the day?

This should be simple. It should be easy. It doesn't have to take a long time to pray. It doesn't require you to change your clothes, to dress up, to workout or sweat, or to give up much of anything.

So if prayer is so simple, so easy, and so readily available, then why is it so hard for so many Christians to develop this very simple commitment, the commitment to authentic, daily, regular prayer?

I think it is challenging for a few reasons:

1) *Praying isn't natural* for us, especially when we are not in an obvious crisis. *Prayer is a supernatural,*

spiritual practice, and most of us don't take time to ponder the spiritual things and their value often. Using the methods in this book will help us to make prayer more natural and more focused.

2) Effective prayer is a skill that has to be taught and learned. We don't just pick up the practice of effective prayer without any mentoring or training. The vast majority of Christians haven't had effective prayer mentors. Again, the methods in this book teach prayer methods that are simple and effective.

3) We don't fully understand the truth that our authentic prayers are **always** heard and **always** answered. The method of journaling will provide the needed evidence to sustain and increase our motivation and desire to pray.

4) We don't fully appreciate the infinitely vast wisdom of God, nor do we recognize just how close and available God is to us.

5) The effects of prayer are not always immediate. The spiritual world lies outside our physical time. We do not realize that when our prayers are sent up, they are answered quickly, even though we may not see or experience the answer until a future date. Again, journaling our prayer requests, convictions, and response dates assists with this.

6) Our struggle with prayer is actually a struggle with faith, as well as a struggle against the spiritual forces which are aligned against God's kingdom. This unseen battle is the true battle. Our fight is to remain

within God's will; while when we are complacent, the enemy is able to catch us off guard. (Ephesians 6:12; Ephesians 4:27).

Action:
The next time you think, "I am too busy to pray today, or I am too tired to pray today, or I don't really have any issues to pray about today;" tell those thoughts to stop!

Instead, replace those thoughts and replace the temptation to skip prayer with the truth of how powerful prayer is. Tell yourself these motivating statements of truth instead:

I can't imagine all that the Lord has for me! I want to receive His will for me! What if I were to miss it because I didn't ask for it in prayer? I will make time to connect with the Spirit of the Lord, to receive what He has for me, to ensure I am in His will today, and to gain the wisdom I need for the day.

Remind yourself, *I don't think I have any issues or problems right now, but I don't know what is around the corner. I will take time to pray and to rely on the Holy Spirit to pray for the things I don't even know will be coming. In this way, the Holy Spirit may send requests for me, even for future things I don't know I will be facing; the Spirit may prepare me for those things through his intercession through my prayers.*

Finally, *imagine your prayers literally lifting up from heaven, affecting the decisions and abilities of the angels and the Holy Spirit to intercede on your behalf. Except, know that it is not just imagination. Your prayers do rise up to the heavens to be heard by the Lord.*

7
Powerful Prayers and Powerful Faith

Why is prayer so powerful? If God knows everything, why doesn't He intercede for us whether we pray or not? Why must we even pray?

The answer: It is actually faith that brings the power of the Lord in our lives. As the verse below in Hebrews 11 explains, *prayer is powerful* not merely because it is communicating with God; but *because it is an act of faith. Prayer is an act of seeking God*; and the verse in Hebrews explains that God rewards those who are earnestly seeking Him.

"And without faith, it is impossible to please God, because anyone who comes to Him must believe that He exists and that he rewards those who earnestly seek Him." - Hebrews 11:6

We can say we have faith; but our actions are louder than our words. If we say we have true faith; but we do not spend much time in prayer – how strong is our faith? If we say we have faith; but we do not spend much time in prayer, we are revealing that we are actually double-minded in our faith. When we do this, we must be honest with ourselves that we are merely "talking the talk;" and not truly walking the walk of faith.

Prayer is not simply changing our attitude or changing our thoughts.

Prayer is not just a way to meditate stress away.
Prayer is not just whispered or spoken wishful thinking.

Prayer is an act of faith. It is a way to earnestly seek the Lord and His ways. Our prayers and our persistence in prayer is an outward measure of our faith in God and our belief that we are truly in relationship with Him. Our prayer life is evidence of our trust in God's promises to us.

Prayer is also an act of obedience; and by obeying the Lord, *we once again demonstrate our faith.* God has commanded us to pray. We obey the Lord in many things; but why do we forget to obey Him in this most simple of things – persistence in prayer?

God commands us to pray because through prayer, we connect with the Spirit.

Through prayer we seek Him.

And those who seek Him are drawing nearer to Him.

Persistent prayer is integral to our spiritual purification, or sanctification, progress.

Prayer is the most influential activity of spiritual formation that will change us to become more like Christ.

It is commonly known that when a person says one thing, yet does another...that there is duality in his heart and mind. We know that "actions speak louder than words." Jesus similarly said, "By your fruits you will know them." What Jesus meant was that you will know his true followers by how they behave. Do they behave in ways that show they are more Christ-like, or do they behave in ways that are more world-like?

If someone were to ask you, do you believe in the power of persistent and regular prayer? What would you say in response?

Do you believe you have the ability to communicate with the all-powerful God, creator of the universe?

Do you believe that the Holy Spirit will intervene for you; not only in the things you pray about, but also on issues you don't even know you should pray about?

Do you believe that God is waiting for you to call on Him, just waiting for an opportunity to answer your prayer in accordance with His will?

Do you truly want to seek His will? Do you truly believe His will is what is best and most exciting for your life?

Now reflect on your actual prayer life. Do your actual prayer patterns provide evidence that supports what you say you believe about God and prayer? Or do your actions actually reveal a double mind within you?

These are the types of questions we don't really want to ask of ourselves. It's easier just to move along, doing what we have always done. After all, our friends and family members are probably not going to point out the fact that what we say and what we do in regards to prayer doesn't match up. Our friends in church probably won't confront us about it either. That wouldn't be polite of them.

Yet these are the same questions we must ask and resolve if we want to experience a spiritual breakthrough.. *To have a spiritual breakthrough we must search ourselves, with the help and guidance of the Holy Spirit, and allow ourselves to be purified and to become unified in who we say we are, what our face is to the public, and what our actions truly are.*

The world looks on the outside appearance. But the Lord looks on the heart (1 Samuel 16:7). Likewise, we can dress up our "outside appearance" by speaking and claiming that we believe in the power of prayer, while our actions may reveal that our beliefs really aren't as strong as we claim them to be.

The Bible verse in Hebrews states that "anyone who comes to Him must believe that He exists." I posit that the opposite is also true. Anyone who does not come to Him regularly does not truly grasp the truth that He is there, listening, with a promise to respond.

So do you truly believe in the power of God and the promise of His guidance if you pray and seek Him? Do you truly believe that God answers your prayers – all of them?

Then why are you trying to manage so much of your life on your own? Take it all to Him!

He <u>doesn't</u> say to us, "*If you are overburdened, give some of the heavier tasks to Me and I will lighten your load.*" No, instead, we are blessed to be commanded to bring *all* our requests to Him. (Phillipians 4:6). *All!* That means bring it all to Him -- everything, the totality of it!

Action:
Take a personal inventory of your actual prayer life. Write down the answers to these questions. When do you pray? Where do you pray? What types of things do you pray about? What do your actions reveal about your true heart with regard to your beliefs on prayer? What changes will you make, starting today, so that your prayer life will reflect your true heart towards God and His availability to you through prayer?

Finally, at the end of this book, in the Resources Section, you will find a number of Psalms journal prompts and other guides to help you in your quest to be closer to God. Use these resources or create your own.

You may have reached the end of this book; but you now have the methods and tools to be at the beginning of the next level in your journey of faith with the Lord.

Let's use these strategies regularly so that we may draw near to God and receive the promise that He, in return, will draw near to us!

Resources

THE 4 STEP PRAYER

1) Begin prayer with thanks and praise to God

2) Next, confess to the Lord all that comes to mind, *and intentionally accept His forgiveness.*

3) Next, make your prayer requests to God – for yourself and for others.

4) Finally, close your prayer by authentically releasing the outcome of the prayer to God's will and his plan. Let God know you will accept the result because you trust His plan is best.

Journal Pages for Praying the Psalms

Psalm 119:33-38

Write the verses from the Psalm in your preferred translation:

Write your prayer, patterned upon this Psalm, in your own words:

Psalm 121:1-8

Write the verses from the Psalm in your preferred translation:

Write your prayer, patterned upon this Psalm, in your own words:

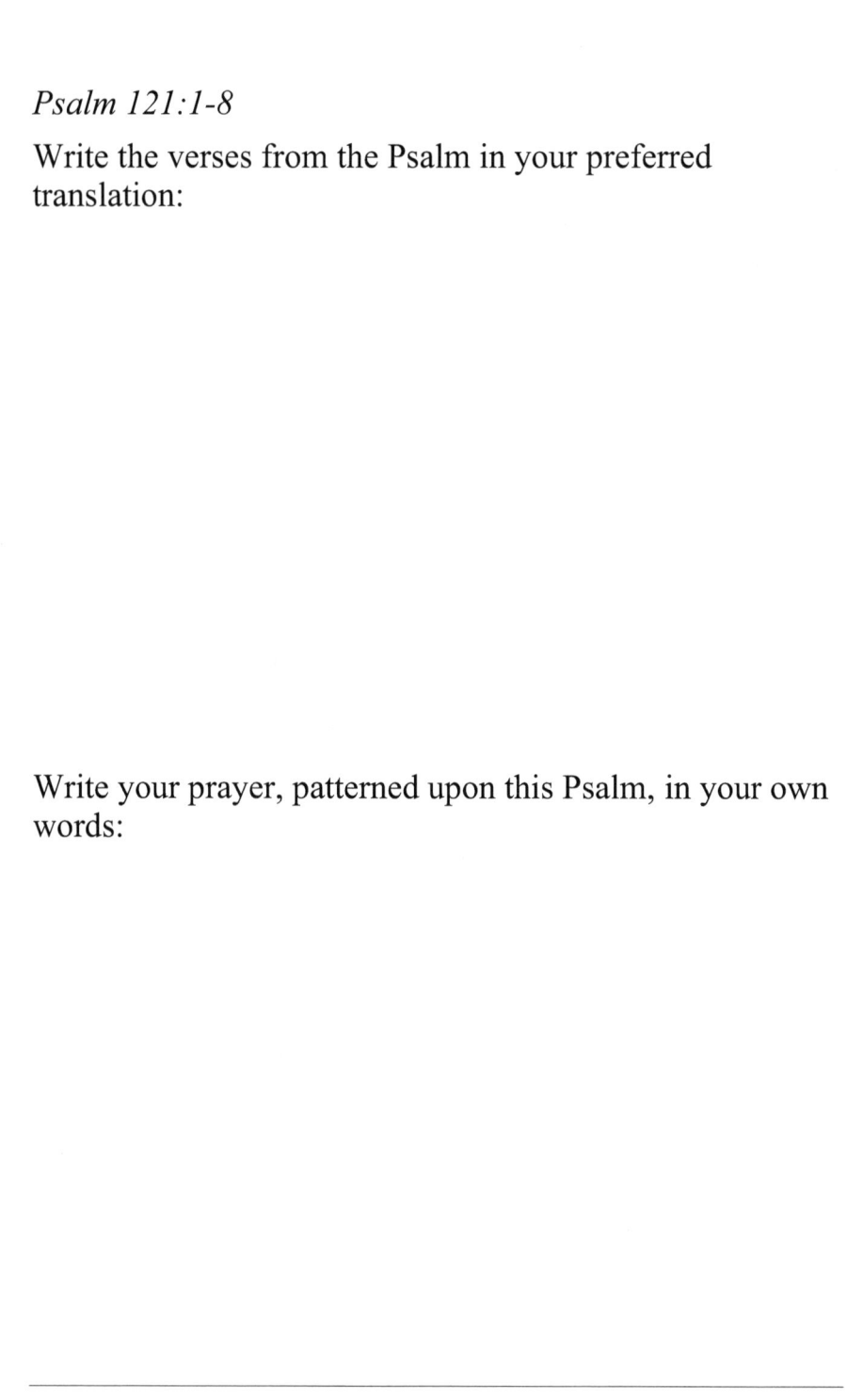

Prayer Journal

Date	Request	Answered Date	Notes

About the Author

To find all the author's titles, go to to Amazon.com

and use a search for "Sherry Elaine Evans"

Sherry is the founder and principle author of the Gospel Life Learning blog where she writes at http://www.gospellifelearning.com. She interacts with her readers on her facebook page: https://www.facebook.com/GospelLifeBooks and she has recently begun tweeting at https://twitter.com/gospellifelearn .

Sherry lives in Spring, TX. Studying the Bible -- in depth -- has become one of her life's greatest passions. In 2011, Sherry began expanding her Bible study notes into full length books and publishing them under Gospel Life Publishing. Sherry graduated Baylor University (BA) and University of Houston (MA). At the time of this books publication, she is completing graduate studies in Biblical Studies & Biblical Languages through New Orleans Seminary. Through her Bible studies and books, Sherry desires to share and motivate others to seek and experience the joy of living daily close to Him.

BONUS CONTENT

from the Author

4 Days of Excerpts from

He Called: 56 Daily Studies and Reflections with the Words of Christ

By Sherry Elaine Evans

Day 1
Jesus Calms the Storm

That day when evening came, he said to his disciples, "Let us go over to the other side." Leaving the crowd behind, they took him along, just as he was, in the boat. There were also other boats with him. A furious squall came up, and the waves broke over the boat, so that it was nearly swamped. Jesus was in the stern, sleeping on a cushion. The disciples woke him and said to him, "Teacher, don't you care if we drown?"

He got up, rebuked the wind and said to the waves, "Quiet! Be still!" Then the wind died down and it was completely calm. He said to his disciples, "Why are you so afraid? Do you still have no faith?" They were terrified and asked each other, "Who is this? Even the wind and the waves obey him!"

Mark 4: 35-41

In this passage of Scripture, Jesus says, "Why are you so afraid? Do you still have no faith?" Think about that for a minute. Is Jesus suggesting that the presence of fear is an indicator of lack of faith? It certainly seems so. And yes, it is true, being fearful or anxious,

although a normal reaction to many life events, does indicate a lack of faith that God is in control and His will is being carried out.

However, it is also important to notice that even though the disciples were afraid, and even though they were assuming the worst as if they were going to die, that *Jesus still helped them*. Jesus still met their needs, and calmed them, and calmed the storm. The next time an event like this would happen, I'm certain that the disciples would demonstrate a stronger faith with less fear.

Even if you are afraid, very afraid, about a life situation, you can still go to Jesus in prayer with your fears. Your fear does indicate lack of complete faith, but at the same time it is a normal human reaction, and God will still answer your prayer and calm you in the process. Each time that you face a similar stressful or fearful situation, you will find yourself better able to rely on God, and you will find that you succumb less to fearful thoughts. You will waste less time in anxiousness. Being able to stay calm (or calmer than before) during stressful times is a process of spiritual maturity. The ability to be calmed within the storm around you demonstrates how God his working in you.

Application Scenarios (with journal prompts in bold):

What are some life scenarios that currently cause you to have fear and anxiety about the future? Are you worried about money or meeting your financial

obligations? About the economy? Are you concerned about another person – their health, their lifestyle? Perhaps you actually have a diagnosed panic or anxiety disorder. What about relationships? Do you worry that you will lose precious relationships or that perhaps you won't find a meaningful relationship? What scenarios in your life bring you anxiety or fear? **Take 2 to 3 minutes, and quickly write as many things down that you can think of that cause you anxiety or fear.**

Next, take that list to God in prayer. Confess your anxiety before God and ask for His peace in that area of your life. You can pray specifically, *"God, I bring my fear to you about* _____. *Help me to recognize that you are in control and that I can trust you. Strengthen my faith and trust in you. Please remove these anxious and fearful feelings from me and replace them with your peace and a portion of your wisdom."* Pray that simple prayer over again, for each item on your list.

Day 2.

Jesus Heals a Demon-Possessed Man

They went across the lake to the region of the Gerasenes. When Jesus got out of the boat, a man with an impure spirit came from the tombs to meet him. This man lived in the tombs, and no one could bind him anymore, not even with a chain. For he had often been chained hand and foot, but he tore the chains apart and broke the irons on his feet. No one was strong enough to subdue him. Night and day among the tombs and in the hills he would cry out and cut himself with stones.

When he saw Jesus from a distance, he ran and fell on his knees in front of him. He shouted at the top of his voice, "What do you want with me, Jesus, Son of the Most High God? In God's name don't torture me!" For Jesus had said to him, "Come out of this man, you impure spirit!"

Then Jesus asked him, "What is your name?"

"My name is Legion," he replied, "for we are many." And he begged Jesus again and again not to send them out of the area.

A large herd of pigs was feeding on the nearby hillside. The demons begged Jesus, "Send us among the pigs; allow us to go into them." He gave them permission, and the impure spirits came out and went into the pigs. The herd, about two thousand in number, rushed down the steep bank into the lake and were drowned.

Those tending the pigs ran off and reported this in the town and countryside, and the people went out to see what had happened. When they came to Jesus, they saw the man who had been possessed by the legion of demons, sitting there, dressed and in his right mind; and they were afraid.

Those who had seen it told the people what had happened to the demon-possessed man—and told about the pigs as well. Then the people began to plead with Jesus to leave their region.

As Jesus was getting into the boat, the man who had been demon-possessed begged to go with him. Jesus did not let him, but said, "Go home to your own people and tell them how much the Lord has done for you, and how he has had mercy on you." So the man went away and began to tell in the Decapolis how much Jesus had done for him. And all the people were amazed.

Mark 5:1-20

Here we have a true story of how Jesus healed a man of demon possession. This man experienced first-hand the power of Jesus through a personal miracle. Afterwards, naturally, the man wanted to go and be with Jesus. In fact, the story says that the man was begging Jesus to let him join Him! But Jesus had another plan for this man. Jesus gave the man an order. He told the man to immediately go and give his testimony to others. The man was to go right away and

tell about how the power of the Lord completely restored his life.

Let's go back and look at the first part of this passage for a minute. Notice how much description Mark gives us to describe how possessed by evil this man was. This man was so out of control, that the people in town had actually kept him chained up near the cemetery! When the man broke out of his chains, he still could be heard wailing and crying from the outskirts of town. The people of the town had obviously completely given up any hope for this man's future. He was a complete outcast. He was as good as dead; he was literally living among the graves of the dead. But Jesus cured this man with his words, with a powerful command.

After the man was healed, Jesus then immediately sent the man on a mission! Jesus didn't tell the man to go study the scriptures first, or to meet with the local believers for a Bible study. Jesus didn't tell him to enroll in the local seminary before he started his mission work. Jesus told him to go right away

and tell his story to others! This incident reveals how God is able to take the "most messed up person" in town, instantly change that person, and then immediately use that person for His work! This man, after he was healed, did what Jesus commanded. He went back to tell how he came face to face with Jesus and all his demons were cast out. He *was immediately restored*; and he *was immediately effective for the*

kingdom.

Application Scenarios (with journal prompts in bold):

Every Christian has at least one significant testimony of how God has worked in their lives. God wants us to share our personal testimonies with others. "Go...and tell them how much the Lord has done for you and how He has had mercy for you," Jesus commanded. Your testimony may or may not be about your "conversion" experience, such as when you met the Lord and became a Christian. It is more likely that your most effective report on God's work in your life is about how He brought you through a difficult time; or how He has blessed you even though you didn't

deserve it in the least. Your testimony may likely be about how God took an extremely negative event in your life and turned it around and created something good from it.

Take some time today with your journal . **Write down at least one major event in your life where you clearly felt or knew that God was working for you. Specifically, write down something he has done for you that has shown his mercy upon you.** Then think of this: how would you share that testimony with someone else? We are instructed in I Peter 3:15 to *"always be prepared to give an answer to everyone who asks you to give the reason for the hope that you have. But do this with gentleness and respect."* By putting your testimony (or testimonies) in writing for your own clarity, you are preparing yourself according to Peter's instruction. Sharing your own personal testimony and experience with God is also a "gentle and respectful" way to share the good news of Christ's work, just as Peter instructed. And let me also say this: once you have your testimony thought out and put into words – be ready! When you have your testimony of God's mercy and hope prepared and on the tip of your tongue, you will likely find that God puts obvious opportunities right in front of you to share your testimony with others! When you are prepared, expect that God will use you! Pray for such opportunities because they are exciting and amazing when they occur. Such "God-appointed" opportunities will also serve to strengthen your faith. When such opportunities "spontaneously" occur, they become further evidence to you of the reality that the almighty God knows you personally, and is using your life and experiences to expand his kingdom.

Day 3.
Jesus Heals the Bleeding Woman

A large crowd followed and pressed around him. And a woman was there who had been subject to bleeding for twelve years. She had suffered a great deal under the care of many doctors and had spent all she had, yet instead of getting better she grew worse. When she heard about Jesus, she came up behind him in the crowd and touched his cloak, because she thought, "If I just touch his clothes, I will be healed." Immediately her bleeding stopped and she felt in her body that she was freed from her suffering.

At once Jesus realized that power had gone out from him. He turned around in the crowd and asked, "Who touched my clothes?"

"You see the people crowding against you," his disciples answered, "and yet you can ask, 'Who touched me?'"

But Jesus kept looking around to see who had done it. Then the woman, knowing what had happened to her, came and fell at his feet and, trembling with fear, told him the whole truth.

He said to her, "Daughter, your faith has healed you. Go in peace and be freed from your suffering."

Mark 5:24b-34

Miracle healings and recoveries such as these still happen regularly today. They happen all the time, every day. People ask, "Why doesn't God do miracles today?" The answer is this: He does do miracles all day, every day! But people want to explain them away somehow. God may not have given *you* a miracle lately; but He is definitely working all over the world. I am referring to quiet healings that occur when a person goes to God, through the name of Jesus, in faith, and when the person asks others of faith to pray, in person, with them.

Almost every Christian I know, can tell of someone who was healed even though highly trained medical doctors had projected a very poor prognosis with hardly any chance of recovery. If you do not know of such a story within your own circle of acquaintances, then all you have to do is go to an internet search to find examples of God working such miracles all over the world! In fact, I just went to google.com and searched the news articles. I searched for the words *miracle recovery*. Over 9000 findings turned up – and these are just the ones that have been published in the news-related outlets over the past few months! Of course, there are many millions more that are "lesser miracles" that never get published. You can even do an email alert and the Google program will send you an email every time a new story about a miracle recovery is published. Your email box will literally bemaxed-out and flooded with miracles!

With all that said, let's now return back to the Bible passage for today, about the bleeding woman in the crowd. The woman who was healed in Matthew 5 demonstrated active faith. Do not underestimate the level of active faith this lady demonstrated. She had been bleeding internally for 12 years! How fatigued and tired and "run down" she would have felt after having been ill for so long. Yet she left her home and went out to meet Jesus. She pushed her way through the crowd. How she must have struggled to keep up with the crowd! Yet she actively reached to Jesus and touched his cloak with faith! That is active faith.

Active faith. I write the two words again because active faith is the most powerful tool a Christian can have in life. Active faith. When you wake up each morning, make a commitment to have active faith throughout the day. Your life will transform!

But what is active faith? Most of us don't have time in the day to go out and volunteer for others or demonstrate active faith, right? Wrong! Active faith is very simple. I think the devil himself, the great deceiver, has allowed us to believe that demonstrating active faith is a whole lot harder and more time consuming than it actually is. Why would he do this? Because the devil knows that active faith is the strongest tool a Christian can develop for the purposes of Christ and the kingdom of God.

If you study the words of Jesus in the entire book of Mark, you will learn that active faith is the faith that enables you to "see God" working in you and around

you. In my first book of this series, titled *Discovering God's Will: Day by Day Journey by the Words of Jesus,* I discussed extensively how God's will for our lives is for us to come to him daily and to demonstrate active faith. For some reason, just having "general belief" in God is not enough to really unveil the works God is doing in and around you on a regular basis. ***It is the person with active faith that sees God's work.***

The best news is that active faith is really quite simple. Active faith is merely coming to God, and allowing yourself to be touched and refreshed in your relationship with Him. We frequently complicate the idea of active faith in our churches. We think, and sometimes we are instructed, that active faith means we are volunteering somewhere in our community or in our church. That belief isn't biblical. There are many instances in the New Testament where people were praised for their great faith. In every instance, the action they were praised for was this: they believed enough to actually come to Jesus and to ask Him for help. So how do we demonstrate active faith today? Quite simply, we demonstrate our faith through *daily prayer.*

The quality of our prayer life is probably the number one indicator of our level of active faith. We are told over and over again by Christ, and then later by his disciples, that we should bring **all** of our concerns to God. Sounds easy, right? It is easy. But did you know that surveys show that only a fraction of people who call themselves Christians actually pray to God daily? I can tell you this: you will not have the privilege of seeing God working around you if you do not have a regular, meaningful prayer life. And the converse of that is true too – it is through an active prayer life that we are enabled to see the very active works of God around us.

Application Scenarios (with journal prompts in bold)

Until now, what has the term *active faith* meant to you? What did you learn today about what active faith was, and is, to Jesus? Are you capable of demonstrating active faith on a daily basis? How do you think your life might transform if you do?

Do you take all your concerns to God daily? Or do you fret and stress for hours or even days first? Do you wear yourself out before you finally realize you need to talk to God? I will admit that I still frequently tend to overreact and "stress-out" first, and then pray later! I do this even though I definitely know I should go to God first. Taking our concerns directly to God is not necessarily basic human nature. When we do take all our issues and concerns to God on a regular basis, however, we slowly develop a new nature – one that is more sensitive to God's presence around us, even in our day to day activities.

Day 4.
Jesus Resurrects a Daughter

Then one of the synagogue rulers, named Jairus, came there. Seeing Jesus, he fell at his feet and pleaded earnestly with him, "My little daughter is dying. Please come and put your hands on her so that she will be healed and live." So Jesus went with him.....

... While Jesus was still speaking, some people came from the house of Jairus, the synagogue leader. "Your daughter is dead," they said. "Why bother the teacher anymore?"

Overhearing what they said, Jesus told him, "Don't be afraid; just believe."

He did not let anyone to follow him except Peter, James and John the brother of James. When they came to the home of the synagogue leader, Jesus saw a commotion, with people crying and wailing loudly. He went in and said to them, "Why all this commotion and wailing? The child is not dead but asleep." But they laughed at him.

After he put them all out, he took the child's father and mother and the disciples who were with him, and went in where the child was. He took her by the hand and said to her, "Talitha koum!" (which means "Little girl, I say to you, get up!"). Immediately the girl stood up and began to walk around (she was twelve years old). At this they were completely astonished. He gave strict orders not to let anyone know about this, and told them to give her something to eat.

Mark 5:22-24a, 35-43

There are many paths I could take in digging out deeper meanings in this passage. One aspect of this bible account that just jumps out at me is this: Notice who was able to directly witness the miracle of Jairus' daughter's

resurrection. Also notice which group of people *were not allowed permission* to see this miracle firsthand.

This is one of the few miracle accounts where we are told that Jesus actually excluded some individuals from being able to watch the miracle occur. As Jesus was speaking and walking, some friends of Jairus came out and announced, "Your daughter is dead....there is no reason to bother the teacher anymore." These people already determined that Jesus couldn't do anything now. They assumed that Jesus' power was not great enough to overcome the finality of death. Because they placed limits in their beliefs as to how much Jesus could actually help, they were excluded from viewing the miracle take place. Notice that as Jesus traveled with Jairus back to Jairus' home,

that he did not invite these friends of Jairus to come with them. He only allowed Jairus and the disciples who were with him to come and witness the miracle. The passage here clearly states that Jesus "did not let anyone follow him except Peter, James, and John."

So the first group of people who were excluded from witnessing Jesus' miracle were those who had assumed Jesus wouldn't be able or willing to help. They assumed the situation had grown too dire and that there was no hope remaining.

Then, there is a second group of friends whom were also excluded from witnessing the miracle first hand. Mark tells us that when Jesus entered the house, he stated, "The child is not dead, but asleep." However, most of the people in the home laughed at Jesus. The story goes on to tell us that Jesus "put them [the scoffers] out" of the home before he performed the miraculous resurrection of Jairus' daughter.

It is very clear, then, that the ones who saw the miracle were the ones

a) who had a trusting relationship with Jesus (the disciples), and

b) those who initiated a relationship with Jesus by approaching Him with faith and trust.

Jairus (and his wife) trusted Jesus could help. When Jesus told Jairus he could still help, even after the death of his daughter, Jairus trusted Jesus' words. And Jairus witnessed an amazing miracle that very day!

Don't be afraid; just believe, just trust me. These essentially were Jesus words to Jairus. These are also his words for us today. You must have faith and trust to experience first hand miracles. Naturally, those who assume there are limits to Christ's power, and those who scoff at Jesus, will not be able to see or discern the works of the Lord around them.

Application Scenarios (with journal prompts in bold):

What problems or difficulties are you currently facing or have you faced in the past?

Have you seen the hand of God working through your difficult times? If not, why do you think you haven't been able to? Have you assumed God wouldn't do what you asked? Have you assumed He wouldn't take an interest in your difficulties?

Have you been afraid to "bother God?" Have you actually been skeptical of God's view of how his creation works? If you haven't experienced God in this way, try to determine what is holding you back from experiencing or noticing His works. Perhaps you have doubts about God really wanting to have a relationship with you?

Perhaps you've just assumed God is too busy or not really there for you as an individual. Maybe you simply just don't believe that the Lord really does intervene in life today. Maybe you didn't even go to God in prayer and ask Him to be with you and to work through the situation with you. Now that you have had time to think about it, **write down what your attitude may have been that prevented you from experiencing God during a difficult time.**

On the other hand, **if you have been able to see, or sense the presence of God during difficult times, then make note of what faith based actions you took during that time.** Then keep doing those things, of course, so you may continue to realize the Lord's great works.

Note: To study all of the words and teachings with Jesus, look for the title *He Called: 56 Daily Studies and Reflections with the Words of Christ* by Sherry Elaine Evans, available online at Amazon.com.

Made in the USA
Middletown, DE
14 June 2018